British Columbia

Jill Foran

WEIGL EDUCATIONAL PUBLISHERS

Published by Weigl Educational Publishers Limited
6325 10 Street SE
Calgary, Alberta, Canada
T2H 2Z9
Web site: www.weigl.com

We acknowledge the financial support of the Government of Canada through the Book Publishing
Industry Development Program (BPIDP) for our publishing activities.

National Library of Canada Cataloguing in Publication Data
Foran, Jill
  British Columbia / Jill Foran.
  (Canadian sites and symbols)
  Includes index.
  ISBN 1-55388-023-4
  1. Provincial emblems--British Columbia--Juvenile literature.
2. Heraldry--British Columbia--Juvenile literature. I. Title. II. Series.
CR213.B75F67 2003   j929.6'09711   C2003-910526-1

Printed in the United States of America
1 2 3 4 5 6 7 8 9 0   07 06 05 04 03

Project Coordinator: Heather C. Hudak
Design: Janine Vangool
Layout: Virginia Boulay
Copy Editor: Tina Schwartzenberger
Photo Researcher: Barbara Hoffman

Photograph Credits
Every reasonable effort has been made to trace ownership and to obtain permission to reprint
copyright material. The publishers would be pleased to have any errors or omissions brought to
their attention so that they may be corrected in subsequent printings.

Cover: totem poles (**Al Harvey/The Slide Farm**); **Barrett & MacKay:** page 20; **Trevor Batstone:** pages
3B, 11; **British Columbia Archives:** page 21T; **Corel Corporation:** pages 3T, 9, 12, 13T; **Al Harvey/The
Slide Farm:** pages 4, 7, 14, 15, 17B 18, 21B, 22, 23; **Ray Joubert:** page 10; **Kirk Makepeace/JADE WEST
GROUP:** pages 3M, 16, 17T; **Mary Evans Picture Library:** page 6 inset; **National Archives of Canada:**
page 6 (C-008133); **Provincial Government of British Columbia:** pages 1, 8; **Kenneth G. Ransom:** page
13B; **www.chrischeadle.com:** page 5; **J. Yanyshyn/Visions West:** page 19.

Contents

Introduction   4

What's in a Name?   6

Coat of Arms Closeup   8

Flying the Flag   10

Mammals and Marine Animals   12

Towering Trees   14

Emblems of the Earth   16

A Symbolic Staff   18

Special Places   20

Quiz   22

Glossary/Index   24

Introduction

Canada is a large country. The ten Canadian provinces and three territories cover a vast amount of land. From one province or territory to another, the people, lifestyles, land, and animals are quite different. Each province and territory has its own **identity**. The provinces and territories use **symbols** to represent this identity. This book looks at the symbols that represent the province of British Columbia.

Yukon Territory

Northwest Territories

Nunavut

British Columbia

Alberta

Manitoba

Saskatchewan

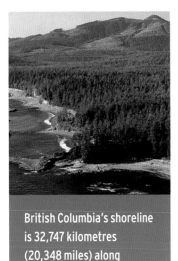

British Columbia's shoreline is 32,747 kilometres (20,348 miles) along the Pacific Ocean.

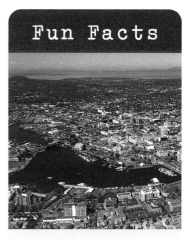

British Columbia is Canada's westernmost province. When people think about British Columbia, they usually think about the province's natural beauty. It has towering mountains, rugged coastlines, and ancient **rain forests**. People in British Columbia are very proud of their province's landscapes and rich history. All of the official symbols of British Columbia are connected to its history and wilderness.

The capital of British Columbia is Victoria, located on Vancouver Island.

About 4 million people live in British Columbia.

Vancouver is British Columbia's largest city.

British Columbia stretches from the Rocky Mountains to the Pacific Ocean.

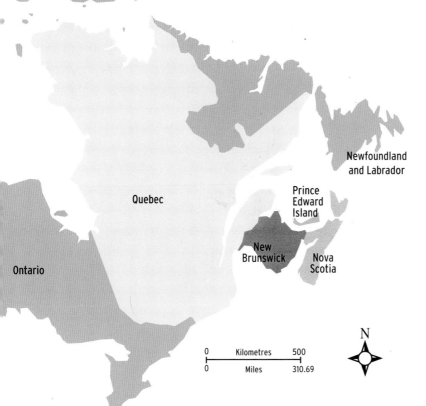

Newfoundland and Labrador

Quebec

Prince Edward Island

New Brunswick

Nova Scotia

Ontario

| 0 | Kilometres | 500 |
| 0 | Miles | 310.69 |

N

What's in a Name?

British Columbia was not always a Canadian province. For many years, it was a British colony. This means it was ruled by Great Britain. The colony of British Columbia was formed in 1858. During this time, the area that made up British Columbia had two names. The northern part was named New Caledonia, and the southern part was named Columbia. At first, British authorities argued over which name to keep, but Queen Victoria made the final decision.

Between 1837 and 1901, Queen Victoria was the official head of state of the United Kingdom and the British Empire, which included Canada.

Queen Victoria wanted to keep the name Columbia. She also wanted to put the word British before Columbia to remind people that the colony belonged to Great Britain.

British Columbia is nicknamed the "Pacific Province." It is the only Canadian province to border the Pacific Ocean. British Columbia's location makes it a gateway to the Pacific and Asia. Other provinces in Canada ship goods to British Columbia's ports to be shipped to Asia and other parts of the world.

The region of Columbia was named for the Columbia River, which flows through the province.

The early colony of British Columbia did not include Vancouver Island. Vancouver Island was a separate colony. In 1866, the two colonies were united under the name British Columbia.

British Columbia joined Confederation on July 20, 1871.

Vancouver is named for Captain George Vancouver. He surveyed the BC coast in 1792 and discovered Vancouver Island.

Coat of Arms Closeup

A coat of arms is a special design that represents a group
or a region. Every Canadian province and territory has
its own coat of arms. British Columbia's coat of arms honours
the province's **heritage**. Each part of the design features symbols
of British Columbia's history and geography.

Fun Facts

British Columbia's shield was designed and adopted long before the coat of arms. It was granted as the province's official shield in 1906.

Queen Elizabeth II granted British Columbia its coat of arms on October 15, 1987.

Features

The lion standing on the crown is the Royal Crest. The lion wears a collar of Pacific dogwood flowers, British Columbia's official flower.

Great Britain's flag, the Union Jack, is on the top half of the shield. It represents British Columbia's past as a colony of Great Britain.

The wavy blue and silver bars and the setting Sun represent British Columbia's location between the Pacific Ocean and the Rocky Mountains.

The stag and the ram represent the early colonies of British Columbia and Vancouver Island.

The wreath and **mantling** beneath the Royal Crest are red and white, the official colours of Canada.

Rams

Dogwood flowers encircle British Columbia's Latin motto *Splendor Sine Occasu*, which means "Splendour Without Diminishment."

Flying the Flag

B ritish Columbia's flag was adopted in 1960. The flag's design copies the shield on the province's coat of arms. The Union Jack is shown on the top part of the flag. The crown in the middle of the Union Jack is a symbol of the province's past as a British colony. The Sun and wavy lines on the bottom part of the flag represent the province's location between the Rocky Mountains and the Pacific Ocean.

Fun Facts

British Columbia's first flag featured the Royal Crest of Great Britain, The letters "B" and "C" stood on either side of the crest.

The Lieutenant Governor's Flag was adopted in 1982.

The Lieutenant Governor's flag is also flown in British Columbia. The Lieutenant Governor is the official representative of the British **monarchy**. The Lieutenant Governor's flag is royal blue. British Columbia's shield is in the centre of the flag. Ten gold maple leaves form a circle around the shield. These leaves symbolize the ten provinces of Canada. The crown above the shield is a reminder that the Lieutenant Governor represents royalty.

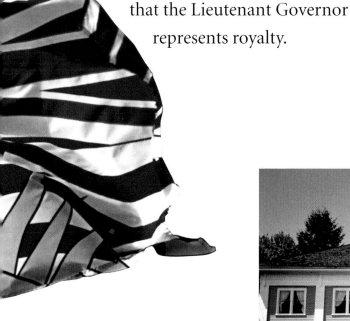

British Columbia's provincial flag is flown in front of many buildings, such as the Fort Langley Community Hall.

Mammals and Marine Animals

British Columbia is home to many animals. The province has more **species** of mammals than any other Canadian province. Animals such as black bears, deer, and elk live in British Columbia's forests. Bighorn sheep, grizzly bears, and mountain goats roam the province's mountain regions. Marine animals such as dolphins, humpback whales, and orcas swim in British Columbia's coastal waters.

Between 120,000 and 160,000 black bears live in British Columbia.

British Columbia is also home to many types of birds. British Columbia's official bird is the Steller's jay, a pretty bird that has a dark blue body and a black head and chest. Steller's jays are most often found on Vancouver Island and in southern British Columbia. They prefer living in forest regions. They hide their nests from predators and can imitate the calls of other birds. Steller's jays often sit on treetops and fence posts to watch over the area. They also steal food from campers and hikers in the woods.

Fun Facts

About 25 percent of the world's bald eagles live in British Columbia.

British Columbia has 17 species of bats, more than any other region of Canada.

The Steller's jay became the province's official bird in 1987. It was voted the most popular bird by the people of British Columbia.

Steller's jays are loud when they are near campsites. They are quiet when they are near their own nests.

Towering Trees

British Columbia's official floral emblem is the Pacific dogwood. The Pacific dogwood can be found in the province's southwestern forests. It grows from 6 to 8 metres (20 to 26 feet) high. In the springtime, beautiful white flowers bloom on the dogwood. In the autumn months, bright red berries grow on the tree. These berries provide food for many birds and animals in British Columbia.

The Pacific dogwood became British Columbia's official floral emblem in 1956.

Fun Facts

The western red cedar got its name from the dark red colour of its bark.

Native Peoples once used the wood of the Pacific dogwood to make bows and arrows. They also used the tree's bark to make dyes. Today, the wood is sometimes used to make piano keys.

In British Columbia, it is against the law to dig up or cut down the Pacific dogwood.

British Columbia has some of Canada's oldest and tallest trees. The province's official tree is the western red cedar. It is found in the moist coastal and interior regions of the province. This **coniferous** tree can grow up to 60 metres tall. Early Native Peoples used the western red cedar to make many items. They made homes from the tree's wood, baskets from its roots, and clothing from its bark. The western red cedar is still used to make furniture, fences, and siding for houses.

Western red cedars can be found in Cathedral Grove in MacMillan Provincial Park. Beautiful hiking trails make the park's forest a popular area to visit.

Emblems of the Earth

Many types of rocks and minerals are found in British Columbia. Jade became British Columbia's official mineral emblem in 1968. There are two different types of jade: jadeite and nephrite. Nephrite ranges in colour from creamy white to green. It is most often olive in colour. Only nephrite jade is mined in British Columbia. It is found in boulders and bedrock throughout the province. British Columbia's Fraser River is the most important source of jade in Canada.

The Kutcho Mine, located near Provencher Lake, is one of British Columbia's main jade-mining areas.

Since 9000 BC, people have used jade to make jewellery and tools. Small pieces of jade are still used to make jewellery. Larger pieces of the gemstone are used for carving. Many artists in British Columbia make jade sculptures and ornaments. This popular mineral is even used to make tiles and tabletops.

Fun Facts

British Columbia is home to some of the brightest, greenest, and hardest jade ever discovered.

Metals mined in British Columbia include copper, gold, silver, and zinc.

British Columbia has the highest risk of earthquakes of any province or territory in Canada.

The tallest mountain in British Columbia is Mount Fairweather. The mountain is 4,663 metres (15,299 feet) high.

A Symbolic Staff

British Columbia's parliament has an official mace. A mace is an ornamental club that is carried as a symbol of authority. It represents the power of the Speaker of the House. When the mace is in place, the province's government has the power to make decisions. British Columbia's mace celebrates the province's British heritage. It has many interesting parts.

Victoria is home to British Columbia's Parliament Buildings. Members of the provincial government have met at these buildings since 1898.

Features

A copy of St. Edward's crown sits on top of the mace's bowl. St. Edward's crown is the official royal crown of the British monarchy.

The mace was handmade from British Columbia silver. It is plated with 24 carat gold.

The deep bowl of the mace is engraved with British Columbia's and Canada's coats of arms.

Four **embossed** scenes also appear on the bowl. They represent British Columbia's forestry, farming, fishing, and mining industries.

Fun Facts

Since British Columbia became a province, the provincial legislature has used three different maces. The current mace was adopted in 1954.

British Columbia has an official **tartan**. It has five colours: blue, which represents the Pacific Ocean; red, which represents Canada's maple leaf; white, which represents the Pacific dogwood flower; green, which represents the province's forests, and gold, which represents the crown and Sun on the shield and flag.

Special Places

Every province and territory has special places that represent its heritage. These places can be a historic fort, a monument, or a park. British Columbia has more than 675 parks and protected areas. These areas include forests, glaciers, islands, lakes, mountains, rivers, and valleys. British Columbia's **landscape** is the most varied of the Canadian provinces. The province is known around the world for the natural beauty of its parks.

Victoria's Thunderbird Park displays west coast totem poles and a replica of a traditional Haida longhouse.

Yoho National Park is one of the most-visited parks in the province. It is located on the western slopes of the Canadian Rockies. This park has scenic lakes, flowing waterfalls, and rugged mountains. The park is also home to some of Canada's oldest rocks and **fossils**. The Burgess Shale fossil beds are found in Yoho National Park. These fossil beds have more than 140 types of fossils dating back 530 million years.

Another popular park in British Columbia is the Pacific Rim National Park on the west coast of Vancouver Island. It has dense rain forests and sandy beaches. **Pods** of gray whales and orcas swim and feed in the coastal waters beyond these beaches.

Alexander MacKenzie trekked across British Columbia. He left his signature on a stone that is now part of Sir Alexander Mackenzie Provincial Park.

The word *yoho* means "awe" in the Cree language

The Gwaii Haanas Reserve is located on British Columbia's Queen Charlotte Islands. The reserve has the world's largest number of ancient totem poles.

The Queen Charlotte Islands are a group of more than 150 islands. Visitors to the islands can watch birds, sea lions, seals, and whales.

Quiz

Based on what you have read, see if you can answer the following questions.

1. What is the capital of British Columbia?

2. Which ocean borders British Columbia?

3. What is British Columbia's most popular bird?

4. Which national park is home to more than 140 kinds of fossils?

A little over a century ago, Vanier Park was the site of a Native village inhabited by the Coast Salish tribe. In the 1960s, it was dedicated as a park.

Answers

8. Nephrite jade

7. The provincial shield

6. Homes, baskets, and clothing

5. A lion, stag, and ram

4. Yoho National Park

3. The Steller's jay

2. The Pacific Ocean

1. Victoria

5. Which animals appear on British Columbia's coat of arms?

6. What items did early Native Peoples make from the western red cedar?

7. The flag of British Columbia is a copy of what design?

8. What gemstone is found in some of British Columbia's boulders and bedrock?

Yoho National Park is open to visitors throughout the entire year. July and August are the best months to visit the park.

Glossary

coniferous: trees that have cones and needles

embossed: a design on a raised surface

fossils: the rocklike remains of ancient animals and plants

heritage: something handed down from earlier generations

identity: the qualities that make a person or thing different from all others

landscape: a stretch of natural scenery

mantling: loose, draping material

monarchy: a nation or state ruled by a king or queen

pods: groups

rain forests: dense forests that receive large amounts of rain

species: a group of animals that are similar and can breed together

symbols: things that stand for something else

tartan: colourful striped patterns that often represent a group of people

Index

coat of arms 8, 9, 10, 19

Elizabeth II 9

Great Britain 6, 7, 9, 11

jade 16, 17

New Caledonia 6

Pacific dogwood 9, 14, 15, 19
Pacific Ocean 4, 5, 7, 9, 10, 19
Pacific Rim National Park 21
parks 20, 21
provincial flag 10, 11, 19
provincial mace 18, 19

Queen Victoria 6

Steller's jay 13

Union Jack 9, 10

Vancouver 5, 7
Vancouver Island 9, 13, 21
Victoria 5, 18, 20

western red cedar 15

Yoho National Park 21